I0880983

SUPER CUTE!

Baby Goats

by Kari Schuetz

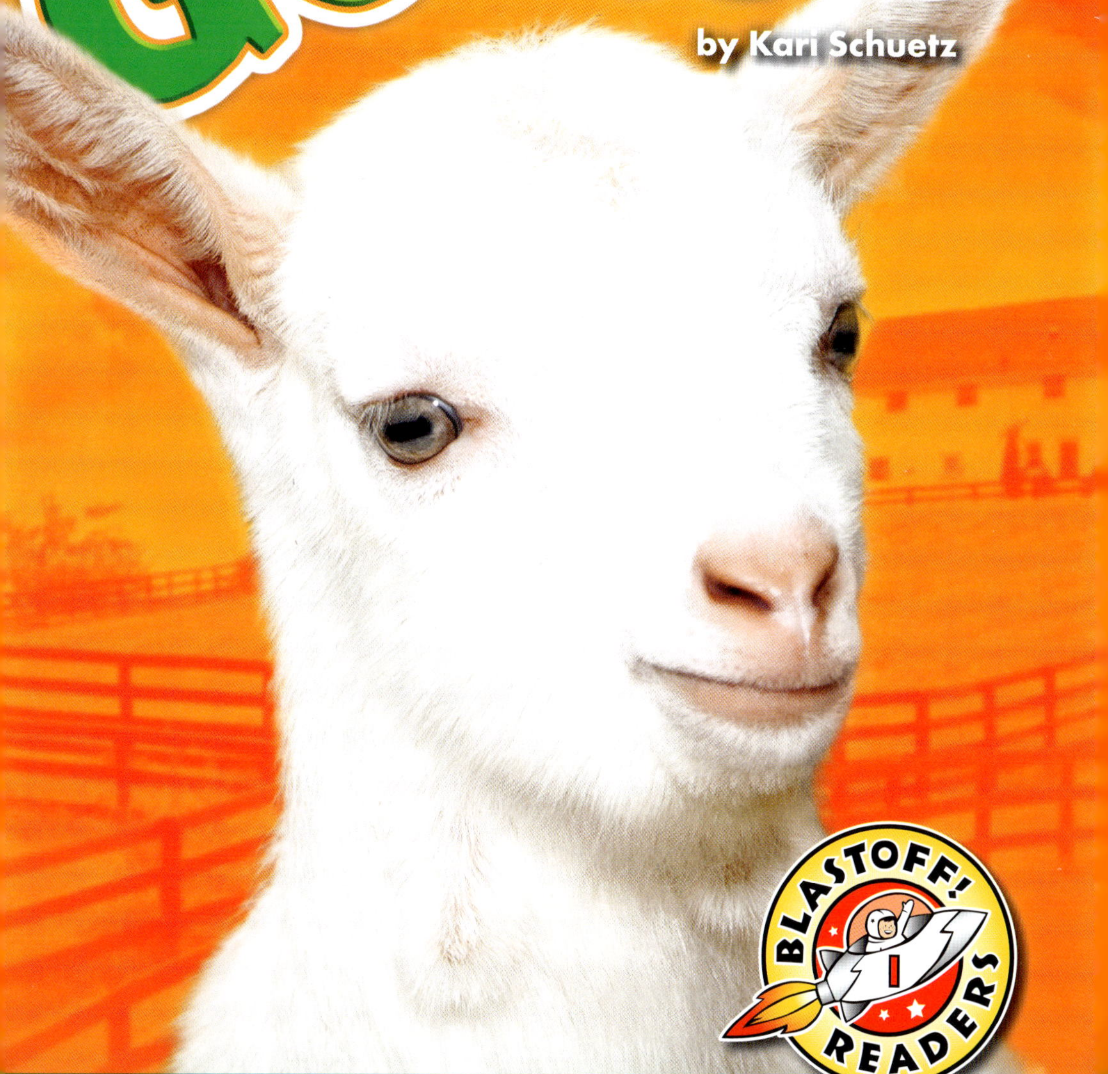

BELLWETHER MEDIA • MINNEAPOLIS, MN

Note to Librarians, Teachers, and Parents:

Blastoff! Readers are carefully developed by literacy experts and combine standards-based content with developmentally appropriate text.

Level 1 provides the most support through repetition of high-frequency words, light text, predictable sentence patterns, and strong visual support.

Level 2 offers early readers a bit more challenge through varied simple sentences, increased text load, and less repetition of high-frequency words.

Level 3 advances early-fluent readers toward fluency through increased text and concept load, less reliance on visuals, longer sentences, and more literary language.

Level 4 builds reading stamina by providing more text per page, increased use of punctuation, greater variation in sentence patterns, and increasingly challenging vocabulary.

Level 5 encourages children to move from "learning to read" to "reading to learn" by providing even more text, varied writing styles, and less familiar topics.

Whichever book is right for your reader, Blastoff! Readers are the perfect books to build confidence and encourage a love of reading that will last a lifetime!

This edition first published in 2014 by Bellwether Media, Inc.

No part of this publication may be reproduced in whole or in part without written permission of the publisher. For information regarding permission, write to Bellwether Media, Inc., Attention: Permissions Department, 5357 Penn Avenue South, Minneapolis, MN 55419.

Library of Congress Cataloging-in-Publication Data

Schuetz, Kari.
Baby goats / by Kari Schuetz.
p. cm. – (Blastoff! readers. Super cute!)
Audience: K to grade 3.
Summary: "Developed by literacy experts for students in kindergarten through grade three, this book introduces baby goats to young readers through leveled text and related photos"– Provided by publisher.
Includes bibliographical references and index.
ISBN 978-1-60014-927-6 (hardcover : alk. paper)
1. Kids (Goats)–Juvenile literature. 2. Goats–Juvenile literature. I. Title.
SF383.35.S345 2014
636.3'9–dc23

2013004887

Text copyright © 2014 by Bellwether Media, Inc. BLASTOFF! READERS and associated logos are trademarks and/or registered trademarks of Bellwether Media, Inc. SCHOLASTIC, CHILDREN'S PRESS, and associated logos are trademarks and/or registered trademarks of Scholastic Inc.

Printed in the United States of America, North Mankato, MN.

Table of Contents

Goat Kids!

Baby goats are called kids. These kids are twins!

Life With Mom

Kids **bond** with mom when they are little.

Mom **nuzzles** her kid. This shows love.

A kid **bleats** when it is thirsty. Mom feeds it her milk.

Time to Eat

Soon a kid **grazes** on plants. Then it chews its **cud**.

Time to Play

Kids like to explore. They run and jump in fields.

Sometimes kids stand on two legs.

Mountain goat kids climb on top of rocks.

Kids also play together. They bite one another and **butt** heads. Ouch!

Glossary

bleats–makes a noise that sounds like a shaky cry

bond–to become close

butt–to hit with the top of the head

cud–food that is chewed again after being in the belly

grazes–feeds on grasses and other plants

nuzzles–rubs with the nose and mouth

To Learn More

AT THE LIBRARY

Bingham, Caroline. *Animal Playtime.* New York, N.Y.: Dorling Kindersley, 2011.

Mortimer, Rachael. *The Three Billy Goats Fluff.* Wilton, Conn.: Tiger Tales, 2011.

Rozinski, Bob. *Glacier Babies!* Helena, Mont.: Farcountry Press, 2009.

ON THE WEB

Learning more about goats is as easy as 1, 2, 3.

1. Go to www.factsurfer.com.
2. Enter "goats" into the search box.
3. Click the "Surf" button and you will see a list of related Web sites.

With factsurfer.com, finding more information is just a click away.

Index

The images in this book are reproduced through the courtesy of: Baronb, front cover; Visuals Unlimited, Inc./ Tom Walker/ Getty Images, pp. 4-5; Gerard Lacz/ Glow Images, pp. 6-7; Michael James Vicencio, pp. 8-9; ARCO/ Ruegner, M./ Glow Images, pp. 10-11; Catalin Petolea, pp. 12-13; Image Source/ SuperStock, pp. 14-15, 20-21; James Hager/ Robert Harding Picture Library/ SuperStock, pp. 16-17; Josh Schutz, pp. 18-19.